The Perfect Man.®

This book is dedicated to Jenny and Merril,
for making us feel like they've really found their
"Perfect Man".

– S.D.G. and D.A.B.

Who is The Perfect Man?

Ahhhh. The search for the *perfect* man.

For most women, it's a quest that begins practically the moment she's born. There, in the hospital nursery, she smiles sweetly at the boy in the next crib. He returns a long, meaningful glance. Then, like most men, he burps, wets himself and screams for someone to bring him his food. And while she may not realize it at the time, she'll soon discover that his type of male behavior never really changes all that much.

But still she searches. Surely, the perfect man must be out there. Somewhere hidden amongst all those plaid sportcoats, hairy backs and bad toupees, there must be *one* perfect man. Someone who will love her. Someone who shares her interests. Someone who won't mind spoonfeeding her ice cream in bed every night for the rest of his life.

Then it dawns on her. Maybe she's asking too much. Maybe her standards are too high. Maybe, in the interest of all mankind, she should be just a little more accepting of people's flaws, and search for that tiny kernel of *inner* beauty that all men must possess.

Naaaah.

Keep looking for that perfect man. After all, even if he doesn't exist, it beats marrying some dork named Herbert who collects bugs and still lives with his mother.

The Perfect Man.™

(He's cute. He's entertaining. And he
always lets you be in control.)

The Perfect Man.™

(He's cool. He's well-rounded. And he actually knows how to use a broom.)

The Perfect Man.™
(He's sweet. He's loaded. And after a
bad day you can twist his head off.)

The Perfect Man™.

(He's romantic. He's cute. And he has
10 zillion frequent flyer miles.)

Ten Places You Won't Find The Perfect Man.™

- ❑ At a Star Trek Convention.
- ❑ Buying a pair of nylon bike shorts.
- ❑ In a live bait shop.
- ❑ Getting a manicure.
- ❑ At a Karaoke Bar.
- ❑ In your Bio-Nuclear Engineering class.
- ❑ In the studio audience of a game show.
- ❑ At a porno movie.
- ❑ In a commune.
- ❑ At an Andrew Dice Clay concert.

The Perfect Man.™

(If he gives you any trouble, you can stick him in the spokes of your bike.)

The Perfect Man.™

(He's attractive. He's funny. And if he
loses his hair, you just put it back on.)

The Perfect Man.™

(He's quiet. He's deep. And best of all,
he left everything to his wife.)

The Perfect Man.™
(He's tall. He's thin. And if a cuter guy calls, you can just leave him hanging.)

American women like quiet men;
they think they're listening.

– Old Proverb

Not all men are stupid. Some are bachelors.

– Anonymous

The Perfect Man.™
(He's romantic. He's sentimental. And)
you can always recycle him.

The Perfect Man.™

(He's faithful. He's romantic. And
you can always leave him in the freezer.)

The Perfect Man.™

(He's rich. He's smooth. And if you need
a friend, you can chew his ear off.)

The Perfect Man.™

(He cooks. He cleans. And the more
you eat, the better he likes you.)

The Perfect Man™
(The Checklist)

By now you're probably thinking, wouldn't it be nice if there was a quick, easy way to determine whether you've found The Perfect Man™? Well, there is. Just use this simple checklist. If your man answers "Yes" to any of the following questions, sorry, he may be great, but he is not The Perfect Man™.

- ❏ Doesn't like your mother?
- ❏ Still listens to the Bee Gees?
- ❏ No hair on head?
- ❏ Lots of hair on back?
- ❏ Excessive snoring?
- ❏ Wears large gold chains?
- ❏ Has several ex-wives?
- ❏ Ever owned a Gremlin?
- ❏ Still has black-light posters?
- ❏ Lives with his mother?
- ❏ Watches golf on TV?
- ❏ Leaves toilet seat up?
- ❏ Still calls his old girlfriends?
- ❏ Tapes Baywatch?
- ❏ Goes to Monster Truck Shows?
- ❏ Can't cook or clean?
- ❏ Ever forgotten an anniversary?
- ❏ Wears black socks with shorts?
- ❏ Comments about your weight?
- ❏ Thinks PMS is all in your head?

The Perfect Man.™
(He can't talk about sports. He can't talk about cars. And best of all, he can't talk about himself.)

The Perfect Man.™
(He's quiet. He's exotic. And he almost always gets your point.)

The Perfect Man.™

(He's quiet. He's sweet. And if he gives you any grief, you can bite his head off.)

The Perfect Man.™

(He's young. He's cute. And he always comes crawling back to you.)

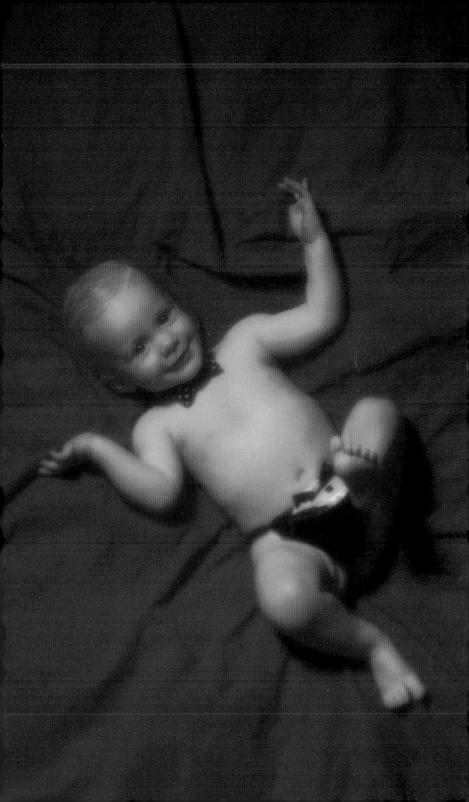

The Perfect Man.™

(He's intelligent. He's sophisticated.)
  And he's really easy to turn on.

Men are like wine. Some turn to vinegar.
But the best improve with age.

– Pope John XXIII

Behind every great man…is a great behind.

– Anonymous

The Perfect Man.™

(He's playful. He's fun. And no matter
what you do, he always comes back for more.)

The Perfect Man.™

(He's famous. He's flexible. And he's always carrying plenty of plastic.)

The Perfect Man.™

(He's smooth. He's well-rounded. And if he looks at another girl, just crack him one.)

The Perfect Man.™
(He's big. He's bright. And he always
goes away in the morning.)

Summer

The Perfect Man.™

(He's happy. He's playful. And he only
pops up when you want him to.)

The Perfect Man.™

(He never snores. Or burps. And if he does, just knock the wind out of him.)

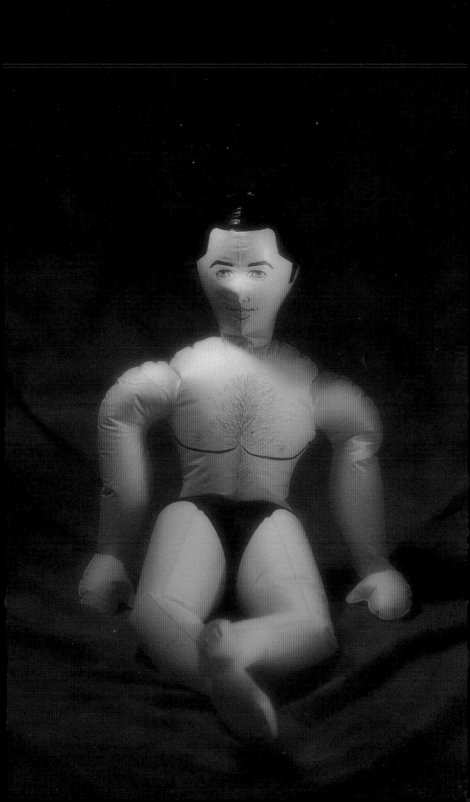

The perfect marriage would be between a blind wife
and a deaf husband.

– Proverb

The one who dies with the most boys wins.

– Anonymous

The Perfect Man.®

(He's cute. He's cuddly. And if he acts up,
you can knock the stuffing out of him.)

Ten Places You Won't Find The Perfect Man.™

- ❏ At a professional wrestling match.
- ❏ At a tanning parlor.
- ❏ Asleep in a Lazy Boy.
- ❏ At a Three Stooges Film Festival.
- ❏ In a rehab clinic.
- ❏ At a nudie bar.
- ❏ At a skeet shooting range.
- ❏ Peeping in your window.
- ❏ On a construction site.
- ❏ At a bowling alley on league night.

ISBN 1-57081-768-5